C000046324

The Ethics of the Letter of James

Greg Forster

Rector of Northenden, Manchester

GROVE BOOKS LIMITED
RIDLEY HALL RD CAMBRIDGE CB3 9HU

Contents

Preface

This book began as a project to survey the ethics of all the Catholic Epistles! I am grateful to members of the Grove Ethics Group for their encouragement, and for their permission to reduce its scope, initially to cover James' and John's Letters, and then just to James. It could still have overrun the allotted 24 pages! Colin Hart was responsible for the previous books in our series on New Testament Ethics, and I am grateful to him both for the example of those books, and his encouragement with this one. He, and the group in general, have seen drafts of it, and improved it with their comments, but should not be blamed for its shortcomings, nor for the opinions (which I have tried to signpost) which do not coincide with received wisdom.

James makes uncomfortable reading. His message for today could simply be 'If you know what is right and do not *do* it, that is a sin!' (4.17) Wealthy, comfortable and wordy churches and individuals need to learn that true faith stands hardship and comes out working. But for James God is central; his are all good gifts, without him business acumen is short-sighted. A modern church which is all action and no creed cannot claim him as mentor! Much of what he wrote retains its force, direct, today. (An audience of American pastors once reputedly wanted to expel the subversive author of 5.1–6 from the country). James would, I think, encourage us to work at how to apply the word in our changed world, but never to hide from its force behind clever analysis.

Earlier ethics booklets by Colin Hart have looked at the ethics of Jesus, the gospels, Paul and the pastorals (see back cover for information).

The Cover Illustration is by Peter Ashton

Copyright © Greg Forster 2002

First Impression January 2002
ISSN 1367-0840
ISBN 1 85174 487 8

1
Introduction

In considering the ethics of a particular book of the New Testament, there is a danger in looking at one author in isolation. James is superficially a 'one off,' but shows strong links with the gospels (especially the supposed source 'Q') and with other letter writers, so that we may legitimately ask what light he sheds on common early Christian moral teaching. We may also ask how he reflects and develops the moral teaching of Jesus, for we are looking in on an ethical process, rather than the ideas of isolated individuals. They are isolated neither from each other nor from their roots in Christ, nor from their Jewish (rabbinic) and Hellenistic background, nor from their successors—the Didache, and the apostolic fathers. How, then, does James relate to his ethical milieu?

Dates and Authorship

Issues of dating and authorship are relevant to discussion of a letter's ethics. For instance, John Robinson sees the appeal to eschatological motivation in James as undeveloped and holds that this reflects the early date of the letter.[1] Is that right, or does it indicate a far later date after ideas of an imminent *parousia* had waned—or is it symptomatic merely of a different strand of church life? Where in this development does the letter come? Further, if there is a family relationship between the author and Jesus, what light might that shed on what he has to say?

What Kind of Ethics?

Ethical teaching can take several forms. At a basic level it is simply a set of imperatives, almost like battlefield orders, relying on the authority of the teacher or his Master. Some modern ethicists have found the NT wanting when it works this way. This is not truly *ethics* since it is not autonomous from an authority figure. At the next level explanation and exhortation are offered. Here too the NT is criticized. Though our writers go to some lengths to exhort and to explain the reasons for conduct, there is still a reference back to authority, and also an internal inconsistency: if I respond to such moral reasoning, I set my conscience above the authority who propounds it, human or divine.[2]

Any discussion of NT ethics should examine the arguments used to support the proposed behaviour, and how they anticipate the categories of modern ethical analysis. Is appeal made to the natural order, to a common sense of right, to

---

1   J A T Robinson, *The Priority of John* (London: SCM Press, 1985) p 341, and *Redating the NT* p 124. Robinson detected a pre-eschatological stage in Christian teaching in John 14, which fell in with his generally early dating of all the NT.

the likely consequences of conduct which from a Christian perspective may be eternal as well as temporal, to some perception of a common good, or to authority and exemplar in one form or another? For example, Peter appeals to the example of Jesus (1 Peter 2.18–25); James cites other exemplars and uses satire, denunciation, irony, and appeals to the nature of things; John appeals for moral consistency, and looks towards spiritual consequences. They answer the question *'why* behave thus?'

Part of our study will consider *what* sort of behaviour an author expects—the range of conduct that he sees fit to highlight, and why he does so. We should also ask how far he moves to a different level of ethics, by offering guiding principles to the readers on which to base their conduct, and from which to consider matters not covered directly. How far does he train his readers *how* to think for themselves ethically (rather than just do what they are told)? Is he preparing people for some degree of ethical autonomy and conscientious decision making, or is he content for them to pursue norms set by the apostles? How far also does the writer try to build communities which will create a moral atmosphere (whatever its basis), supporting moral behaviour and building Christian character? These NT letters are not abstract ethical essays, but are the product of people who are trying (among other things) to *do* ethics with relatively small groups of people in an unsympathetic world—and in this the situation of all except James perhaps contrasts with Jesus' situation in Palestine, where the kingdom of God that he proclaimed might potentially have included all Israel.

And so I shall consider these questions—*how, what, why, where from, for whom, and with whom*—as well as what recent commentators have made of the ethics of James. The ethics of NT writers is a study worthwhile in its own right, rather than just as a sidelight on their theology or soteriology. They came from a Jewish tradition, not discarded by Christ, in which behaviour spoke volumes about where people belonged in relation to God and their community, and which, for all its roots in revealed Torah, was a matter for conscientious choice.

---

2   See, for example, A MacIntyre in *A Short History of Ethics* pp 110–117. Such criticism is valid, however, only if no such authority figure exists and we are not created as moral beings whose conscience should resonate with our creator's. Morality is about the regulation of our relationships with significant others; if God is a significant other in the world he cannot legitimately be ruled out of our ethical thinking! We might also counter that no-one makes every moral decision *de novo*, but builds up his own character on the basis of what he receives and those whom he emulates, as MacIntyre himself recognizes.

2
James—Ethicist or Moralizer?

The letter of James is clearly about Christian conduct. The NEB gives it the title 'Practical Religion,' and its author is scathing about people whose faith does not lead to practical action. Some modern commentators look no further than that. James is simple, basic instruction about how to behave, full stop. Leslie Houlden, for example, begins his section on James in *Ethics and the New Testament* with the sentence, 'The ethics of the epistle of James are, from the conceptual point of view, the simplest in the New Testament.'[3] He finishes the section, eight lines later, 'Even so, in this theologically undeveloped work, the priority of God's action is maintained securely.' Houlden does neither James, nor himself, justice by this brief treatment. Hays is more cursory, though he makes two useful points in passing. In *The Moral Vision of the New Testament* three paragraphs refer to James.[4] He notes that James sees the rich, not Jews or Romans, as Jesus' killers (p 465), and suggests that New Testament ethics uses a 'fruits test' (Matt 7.20). James vehemently affirms that without action faith (or ethics) is dead (p 212).

In part this reluctance to treat James as *ethics* stems from an understanding of ethical discourse which has roots in Greek and Roman philosophy. The stoic Seneca (James' contemporary) searched for a key principle which, if identified, would show him how to act in any circumstance.[5] James superficially does not reveal such a unifying principle but apparently strings together a collection of moral thoughts. However, had James met Seneca he would, I suspect, have offered him the wisdom from above (3.15–17) as the principle, and pointedly told Seneca, rich and influential as he was, to act on it. For him action, not investigation, is the key to ethics.

Those who dismiss James as a mere moralizer do so too lightly. On the contrary, a profound and subtle ethical strand runs through the letter, though masked by a preacher's illustrations and examples of practical outworking. It would go beyond the evidence to say that James sat down to write a treatise on the development of Christian character within a Christian community under stress. But such concern underlies what he says. James should be judged in terms of character or virtue ethics and the corporate construction of the moral life, not the presence or absence of some overriding principle.

---

3   L Houlden, *Ethics in the New Testament* p 66.
4   R B Hays, *The Moral Vision of the New Testament*.
5   W Schrage, *The Ethics of the New Testament*.

James? James Who?

Authorship and dating will affect our understanding of the ethics of James. If 'James' is a cover for some second generation author, then we will read him in a different light from an early apostle. What seems unimaginitive platitude or mere collation of others' wisdom from a second generation author is ground-breaking if this is the first (surviving) attempt to put Christian ethics on paper. In particular, if the faith/works debate in chapter 2 does not belong to discussion in the 50s AD over an open mission to Gentiles then perhaps it is a critique of moral indifference—what the 20th century called 'only-believeism'—stemming from a later misinterpretation of Paul. Sanders sees this rejection of Paul as a stand for ethical independence based on humane values, over against a reliance on texts and received authorities.[6] Sanders' key point is that as an example to show how useless faith without action is, 'James' plucks from the air the responsibility to care for the poor. Since no authority is cited for choosing this case it must have been *self-evident* to him that the poor should be respected and cared for. So, he suggests, 'James' was a daring ethical innovator in trusting his human intuition, rather than a somewhat pedestrian moralist. 'If that assumption ...appears at all likely, then we have come to the most important new point in New Testament ethics, for nowhere else in the New Testament has that principle and that principle alone determined ethical advice' (p 126). If so, he laments, it is only in the faith or works debate that this shows through. In the rest of the letter, except for 1.13–15 where human sin is laid at human, not divine or demonic, feet this 'humanist' strain is lacking and 'James' is conventional though often ascerbic. Yet 'James' in this one innovation offers a pointer to modern Christian ethicists, justifying them in their departure from received wisdom or proof-texts.

Sadly for Sanders' case, James does not so much cite his authorities as internalize them, and this bias to the poor was self-evident because it was an integral part of Jesus' teaching, Old Testament tradition and the best of Rabbinic practice. His readers too would have recognized the allusion, even if they failed to live up to it. In his commentary Mayor noted 71 parallels with Jesus' teaching in the Gospels in 108 verses—more than in all the other New Testament letters together. Several recent studies have highlighted the relationship between James and the elements of gospel transmission.[7] These verbal echoes centre on the Sermon on the Mount, but I note also the emphasis on the poor shared with Luke's Jesus (*cf* 2 Cor 8.18 Gk text, and 20).

If he is late, then comparison with Matthew's treatment of similar material in a similar milieu is instructive. Matthew is held to show an anti-Jewish (if not anti-semitic) tendency, as conflict with the synagogue grew. James, in contrast,

---

6   So Sanders in *Ethics in the NT* pp 115ff.
7   See P J Hartin, 'James and the Q-Sayings of Jesus' or W H Wachob, 'The Voice of Jesus in the Social Rhetoric of James.'

shows sympathy with Judaism, and has been held up as a point of common ground for the church not just with its Jewish roots, but with modern Judaism.

Much in the letter fits best into a first generation (probably Palestinian) Christian setting. Apart from the faith/works discussion there is, for instance, the presence of wealthy landowners within, or on the fringe, of the worshipping community, whose conduct is unreformed by the teachings of Jesus (or even by the Torah itself) (2.1ff, 5.4). This suggests a date before 70AD.[8] If the author is 'apostolic' then he is James the Just, half-brother of Jesus, who led the Jerusalem church until his martyrdom in 62AD. This echoes Matthew's description of his father, Joseph (Matt 1.19).[9]

Tasker is therefore right to raise the possibility that James' near quotation of Jesus' gospel teaching (*eg* 5.12) arises not from literary but from personal contact.[10] He implies that this was during Jesus' ministry, but is it too daring to push this learning process back before then, to when James was growing up in the shadow (or the light) of his brother? Maybe we are reading the product of the same carpenters' bench on which in human terms the teaching of Jesus was lined out. This is conjecture—and to be daring we might ask whether some sayings in *James* are undeveloped *sources* which Jesus polished! Apart from an inherent possibility once the relationship is acknowledged, the only clues come from the antithesis of pride and humility, used in Jas 1.9f and Luke 1.52 (the Magnificat—begging questions as to its source!) but common elsewhere.

James—What Kind of an Ethicist?

Hartin sees James' concern for a moral Christian lifestyle as being in the same tradition as Q, and probably dependent upon it. This lifestyle involves the following of practical wisdom, and aims at perfection (p 214). This wisdom is God's gift, and he notes that where other New Testament writers speak of the Holy Spirit as bringing God's enabling power home to the believer, in James this function is fulfilled by Wisdom (p 175; Jas 1.5, *cf* Luke 11.9–13). Schrage (p 281) notes James' acknowledgement of Wisdom in 1.5, but holds that he does not maintain it as a resource for moral conduct. Hartin in contrast does view it as central; James returns to the theme (3.13–17) in terms reminiscent of Gal 5.22—the 'fruit of the Spirit.'[11] So James does seem to offer a motive force for ethical conduct—he is not concerned just with a list of imperatives. Edgar[12] also sees wisdom in James in this light, as does Davids in the introduction (pp 51–56) to

---

8   The detailed arguments are to be found in Guthrie *New Testament Introduction*, pp 85–88, or Robinson *Redating* pp 118–139 or the commentators, for example, Davids, *The Epistle of James* pp 2–22.
9   For a discussion of James the Just and his significance in the early church, see John Painter, *Just James*. Painter sees this as greater than Luke/Acts and other western traditions allow. See also R Bauckham, 'James and the Jerusalem Church', *Wisdom of James* and *Jude and the Relatives of Jesus in the Early Church*.
10 *The General Epistle of James* p 28.
11 This ties in with suggestions that Jesus is best understood in the Wisdom-tradition, and the personification of wisdom in Judaism (Witherington, *The Jesus Quest* p 194).
12 D H Edgar, *Has God not Chosen the Poor?*

his commentary.

Of recent general studies in New Testament ethics Schrage's pays most attention to James. James' vital concern that faith be realized in living cannot always escape the danger of moralism (says Schrage) but the letter is no mere handbook of morality; truly theological reasons lie behind James' admonitions. In defending James' practical and specific touch he unmasks a further reason why James has been downplayed. New Testament ethics is not so situational as to be vague and contentless. It aims to form actions and communities, and sets up criteria for action, though not necessarily universal norms. It includes specifics, and this should not be forgotten in the Protestant fear of graceless good works (p 10f).

James does acknowledge the place of grace in God's work, but Schrage does not believe that he utilized it as the foundation for his ethics nor that he makes much of Wisdom in this context. Nor does he make the link between the indicative of salvation and the imperative of Christian behaviour in the way found in Paul's writing. Thus baptism (2.7) is a mark of identity, and not a spur to action or character even though gospel and law are part and parcel of the same thing (1.18, 25) (p 281). Thus, though 'no other New Testament document is as dominated by ethical questions as the epistle of James,' and despite some original work in Jas 2.1–3.19, the 'author's purpose is not to be original, but to collect in a kind of catechism what he considers the bare essentials of the Christian life.' The result is, as Dibelius argued, the loose stringing together of injunctions and brief discussions in what the form critics called 'paraenesis' (p 279).

This form-analysis is a further reason why James is undervalued in modern discussions of NT ethics—even Schrage's. With such a label, if an author does try to build on a theme (for instance steadfastness) that is prejudged as repetitiveness, or the use of a catch-word to string his sayings together, while a search for a unifying theme is discouraged. More recent studies have identified other genres from the period, such as the literary letter, exhortations (cf Edgar, p 17, p 34ff) and Jewish sermons.[13] The style of such a sermon was likened to a string of pearls, in which a unifying thread is illustrated by separate examples applicable to different groups among the hearers. Whether this is called paraenesis or something else, its purpose was to socialize the hearers within the culture or society of the speaker to help them internalize the lifestyle being propounded. With this we can agree, without dismissing it as somehow inferior as a way of teaching ethics. Perhaps James has a greater grasp than his detractors of how ethical behaviour is learned.

---

13   J B Adamson, *James, the Man and His Message* pp 104, 112.

3
James' Ethics in the Commentaries

We turn now from writers on NT Ethics to commentators on James. In general Luther's remarks ('a right strawy epistle') and the faith/works issue still influence discussion. Most retain the traditional Introduction-form with its section on the 'Theology of…' where the 'Ethics of James' is more appropriate. In their introductions and their comments on the text they draw attention to sources and parallels for James' language, ideas and methods. Despite his individual approach to all he writes, these parallels are manifold; in both Palestinian and Hellenistic Judaism;[14] in Hellenistic thought (the Stoics, and Philo's Platonism, and to a lesser extent Gnostics); in the New Testament; and in some of the post-apostolic writers (Hermas, the 'Two Ways' in Barnabas and the Didache, and possibly Clement). This is a question of common ambience, not sources, with the exception of Hermas.[15] James comes over as cosmopolitan, despite his address to the '12 tribes of the dispersion.'

Sophie Laws

Laws argues that 'James' is a gentile 'God-fearer' turned Christian (p 38). She places him in Rome in the latter years of the 1st century. He reinterprets traditional Christian teaching for his day. Thus (p 28) James reuses conventional language of the eschatological reward as an incentive to perseverance and morals but relates it not to a messianic 'tribulation' but to everyday hardships suffered by widows (1.27). She also draws attention to James' stress on personal integration. Double-mindedness threatens a Christian's prayers and morals. The hellenistic ideal of oneness receives an ethical dimension, and this, though James never explicitly says so, is in imitation of the God who is One (p 30ff). He juxtaposes God's character and man's, and leaves the reader to draw conclusions. Adamson also noted this trait, for 'James, like Jesus, employed the principle of trajectory; that is he never communicated his teaching exhaustively, but always with a certain reticence leaving the reader to interpret, amplify and apply what he taught' (p 264). I see this as the mark of an ethical educator.

In addition to unity, Laws highlights other ethical interests of James—rich and poor and the uses of speech. James is 'the most consistently ethical document in the NT, but…not based on any theological principle…comparable to…Paul's drawing ethical conclusions from his proclamation of the death and resurrection of Christ in Rom 4. Only in Jas 1.21f is it indicated that the saving

---

14 For example, m Aboth, 1 Macc, 4 Macc, Ecclus, Philo, Test xii Patriarchs; less so the Qumran literature (Laws p 11) with which the contrasts are more significant.
15 Sophie Laws, *Commentary on the Epistle of James* p 22f, arguing that Hermas lifts terminology from James.

word of the gospel carries with it an imperative' (p 27)—a conclusion she backs by quoting Houlden (see above p 5). Characteristic Jewish interests such as circumcision, Sabbath, purity and food are not mentioned, nor is the Rabbinic concept of the *yetsers*. *Dipsychos* (double-minded) is a local idiom.

Though James speaks about the whole law, he actually quotes only the decalogue and Leviticus 19. James is not acquainted with the subtleties of Rabbinic exegesis, such as Paul shows in Rom 4.

J B Adamson

Adamson has written a commentary but his more recent work is a study of 'the man and his message.'[16] Written in the 40sAD well before the Jerusalem council, by the Lord's brother, the letter has a simple theme: 'The teaching of James is simple, like his master's, that the relation of humans to God is a moral one, a way of life, and by obedience to God humans can attain to true life.' (p 32) He looks to Rabbinic rather than Hellenistic models for James' style. The unifying thread is that 'faith without works is dead,' by addressing separate groups in turn with separate illustrations James obscures that (p 112). The controversy about faith and works is not so much theological as ethical (p 67).

Adamson recognizes in James early Christian catechesis such as Carrington and Selwyn proposed.[17] This was possibly a motive for writing in the first place (p 64f), though if so James breaks new ground, and uses motifs not developed later. In discussing some texts, notably 'spirit' in 4.5, Adamson refers to the Rabbinic concept of the two '*yetsers*' or inclinations; the evil *yetser* is a major source of sin, which for James is combatted by wisdom or the gospel torah. It is part of human nature, so that temptation to sin cannot be externalized, though in resisting sin the Christian is resisting the devil. The sources of sin—inclination, pleasures, love of the world, double-mindedness, merely human wisdom, the devil—are part of a single picture (p 343). For James neither sin nor love is abstract—love for neighbour is food and clothing and sin is leaving God out of your business plans.

The letter is bracketed by talk of trial and the endurance for which the hope of the Lord's return gives a reason. But in preparing for the parousia James does not give a timetable, but a jobsheet. For James, 'trials' afflict the people of God, in contrast with the Qumran expectation of affliction for unbelievers. This testing is for the good, but James differs from Qumran, Paul and Hebrews in denying that it is sent by God. He commends endurance, a very Jewish virtue (Ecclus 44.20, 1 Macc 2.52) in the face of these varied trials. Where we distinguish temptation, trial and testing, James sees a combined assault by evil on a person's faith. Endurance leads on to perfection—a recurrent word in James—which is

---

16   *The Epistle of James* and *James, the Man and his Message*.
17   P Carrington, *The Primitive Christian Catechism* and E G Selwyn, *The First Epistle of St Peter* Essay II.

love and faith working out their meaning to the full.

Adamson's assessment of James' ethics is in marked contrast with Laws'. 'James refers to Jesus with equal facility as "the Lord" and..."the Word." The Ethics of James, therefore, goes far beyond Judaistic legalism and approaches the supernatural quality of Pauline ethics in that it takes into account the power which is available for man through Jesus Christ.'[18] This may be overenthusiastic, but Adamson is right to remind us that James does believe that God offers support for those engaged in moral conflict.

Andrew Chester

Like Adamson, Andrew Chester does not write specifically on James' ethics, but on the theology of the letter.[19] He believes it has a coherent theology, looks back in places to Paul, is known by 1 Peter, and stands within the Wisdom tradition in Judaism, which includes consideration of the suffering of the innocent and oppressed poor. Most theories about its date and authorship have inherent problems. There is disagreement over the significance of eschatology in the letter, but the hope of perfection as an eschatological reward is a thread running through. The section on faith in chapter 2 springs out of earlier discussion. For James, works are primary and faith secondary; it only shows up when works are performed. True faith stands the test and comes out working. For Paul justification is the opening step of the Christian life; for James it is the end reward. James' ethics are 'everyday ethics for the faithful...a call to the practice of faith' (p 28). Dibelius' dismissal of James as 'paraenesis... a loose collection of material' 'does not do justice to James as a whole.'

Chester lists James' main points: (i) the misuse of speech, perhaps by teachers of some sort who showed not errors but arrogance (3.1ff, 4.13ff). James urges restraint in the interests of community harmony; (ii) Persistence in the face of suffering, leading to perfection as a reward. (He too notes how for James eschatological tribulation is interwoven with the routine hardships of the disadvantaged in society); (iii) the contrast of riches and poverty, and also pride and humility, which are very prominent in such a short letter. He analyses and exposes power relationships and the causes of conflict, and their folly in the face of life's transience and the final judgment; (iv) love, mercy and humility are cardinal virtues, and since mercy triumphs over judgment it should shape our lifestyle.

James' ethics are social and communal. This is how the community should treat its members, and challenge the world and its standards. Behind such ethics lies a divine precept—gospel or torah. Curiously, Chester calls this 'consequential'—as a consequence of the gracious calling of the word James demands an

---

18   p 274, quoting Henderlite, 'The Epistle of James' in *Interpretation* 3.4, 1949.
19   In *The Theologies of the Letters of James, Peter and Jude*, Andrew Chester and Ralph P Martin.

individual and collective way of life consistent with it. (Contrast Laws, and Schrage quoted above) To follow the law is a delight, and all remains in force— Lev 19.18 is quoted to clinch a point in the argument, not as a general rule, though we might sum the letter up as what love of neighbour means in action. James took the cultic law as read. Wisdom, a practical know-how for life, is a gift of God to be sought, though Chester does not rate it as equivalent to the Spirit as Davids does. At the heart of the community's hardships is the divided nature of the individual. This links with the Jewish concept of the two *yetsers*.[20] He points out that this does not pin down the source of human evil, though all sin (3.2). The remedy is steadfast human resistance, stiffened by the wisdom of God.

Finally, though he thinks James makes sense best if it answers a misrepresented Paul, he warns against assimilating James to Paul. Both, from different circumstances, leave a lesson for the church.

John Painter

John Painter writes about James the man.[21] He takes the letter to be ghost-written after James' death, extending the influence of one who was the key leader of the pre-70 church. He highlights 'theodicy' in the letter, since he sees the real James as an archetypal 'righteous sufferer' (*cf* 5.6) whose own perseverance finds an echo in what 'he' wrote. Painter rejects the idea that 'James' uses the Rabbinic idea of two *yetsers*—rather, evil desire is one aspect of human personality (p 253). He also raises the question of whether the way 'James' ascribes human sin to human desire means that God the creator is ultimately responsible for sin, but concludes that James did not think in such a philosophical way.

Peter Davids

Davids, in contrast, sees the *yetsers* behind the language of split moral personality and desire at the roots of sin in James.[22] He sees the letter deriving from genuine Jacobean material shaped in Palestine but edited and reissued after his death. Its concerns reflect the need for co-operation and unity in a church sorely tested by the political and economic turmoil there prior to the Jewish Revolt (p 34), yet it is a church which might provide a *beth-din*, a local synagogue court, for its wider community (p 109, re 2.1–4, citing W B Ward).

He also prefers to describe theology rather than ethics, for James is offering a framework for understanding and coping with these troubles. The first theological theme he isolates is that of suffering. It is a test, not set by God, which can lead to glory. Eschatology is not the burden of the book, yet it is in the back-

---

20 Citing Marcus, J, 'The Evil Inclination in the Epistle of James' in *Catholic Biblical Quarterly* 44 no 4, 1982, for whom James' *epithumia*, desire, stands for *yetser*.

21 *Just James*. His final chapter 8 deals with the Letter, in relation to James' life, and the early church (p 227ff).

22 *The Epistle of James* pp 36f, 74.

ground and provides the grounds for hope. God's bias to the poor, coloured by the equation in some psalms of poverty and piety, and by Jesus' teaching how hard it is for the rich enter the kingdom, is a major theme. So, of course, is law, grace and faith. For James law is perfect and royal, that is probably 'as interpreted by Jesus,' but he is no legalist; the essence of Christianity is commitment to God in Christ, and the reception of grace from God whose word brings new life. Conflict with Paul is more apparent than real; he uses the key words—faith, works and justification—quite unlike Paul (p 49ff). Wisdom in James should be integrated with these other themes; it is God's gift, a means of overcoming trials and growing virtues, and is practical. Davids does see Wisdom in James as equivalent to Paul's morally empowering Spirit (Rom 7, 8) and the Rabbis' good *yetser* (p 54ff).

Finally, we may note with approval and agreement Davids' introductory point, that James has seen a resurgence of interest in the past quarter century, which he richly deserves (p 1).

4
Grace, Faith and Works and Abraham

The contrast between what James says about faith and works and what is found in Romans and Galatians has shaped attitudes towards his letter since Luther. They *appear* to contradict, if not actually to argue. This appearance is deceptive. Their concerns are different, as Calvin recognized, even if James is 'weak on grace' (see Appendix 1 below).

Paul's concern is that *ritual* 'works of the law' such as circumcision or kosher food are not essential for salvation. He too denounces faith which does not lead to a moral life (Rom 6.1f) and affirms that doers (not mere hearers) of the law are set right with God (Rom 2.13). James is writing about moral law. Though he affirms that the whole law is of equal value (2.10, *cf* Gal 3.10) his examples are moral. He does not even use ceremonial law as an illustration. Paul reinterprets the ceremonials in a moral way (*eg* Col 2.11). For James true religion is visiting the downtrodden.

James and Paul are involved in a wider debate within Judaism about the role of Abraham in salvation. James echoes John the Baptist's theme when he contrasted descent from Abraham and fruit that befits repentance (Luke 3.8). If James antedates Paul that is the precedent to study! He and Paul cite Abraham (differently) as an exemplar of faithfulness, rather than a source of merit, and direct

13

their remarks not against each other but at conventional Jews. ('Faith' in Jas 2.19 is Jewish monotheism, not Pauline faith in the propitiating Christ). The patriarch who in Jewish tradition (John 8) rejoiced to see a vision of the age to come is an example of how a believer reacts. 'Children of Abraham' do what he did (*cf* John 8.39) rather than rest on his laurels.

There is some interaction with Paul in what James says in his ch 2. Not least, the phrase 'by faith alone' seems too close a parallel with Pauline language ('by law alone') for this merely to be different treatment of a quotation also used in 1 Maccabees or Philo. Moo argues that James has heard reports of Paul's teaching, misunderstood by Jewish hearers, before Paul put pen to paper.[24] I read that riddle in reverse.

Our understanding of James is skewed by how we see his relationship with Paul's doctrine of grace. Would we consider James' discussion of faith and works as 'the centre of the epistle' (Schrage, p 282) if it had not been a major Reformation issue? Or would we have treated it merely as one of the pearls on the thread? It flows naturally from what James' says about living out the word. 'Faith' was not invented by Paul. It is an evident part of Jesus' expectations in the Synoptic[25] and Johannine traditions. James is not just to be interpreted with reference to Paul. He addresses people like the lawyer who discussed the 'royal law' and whom Jesus told to *do* likewise (Luke 15).

Without Paul we would see in James someone who knew how Christians' new life depended on God's initiative (1.18) making them a pioneer community who not only *had* the gospel-law, but received from God the wisdom to practice it in adverse circumstances, motivated by an expectation of a final assessment of their lives (4.12, 5.9, see also 1.11, 12), taught by Jesus' vision of a loving community, but weakened by those whose faith was just words. In one short letter can we expect the detail of the Pauline corpus? But God's enabling grace is there, as is the role of the Spirit, seen as divine Wisdom. True, we are not pointed to the 'Christ-event' to motivate our behaviour (Schrage, p 283f, *cf* Phil 2.1ff), nor are we urged to be what we have become in baptism (Rom 6.4). But Schrage's criticism assumes that James is post-Pauline. If Paul had not yet developed the convoluted persuasiveness of Romans, can we find James at fault?

---

24 D J Moo, *The Epistle of James*, p 27ff, 33ff.
25 The idea that hearing the word should lead to fruitful action is found in the parable of the sower, echoed in James. I wonder also how much the incident in Mark 3.31ff, when Jesus' family looked for him, to be told that those who do the will of God are his brothers, was burned into James' conscience?

5
What James Leaves Out—And Puts In

With a work as short as James it is unfair to make too much of what is omitted, but it may indicate what the author saw as important for the communities for whom he wrote. I say 'communities' judiciously. James chooses to focus on public morality. He is concerned that his readers do avoid anger (1.20) and keep unstained from the world (1.27), and alludes to vile practice (3.16), but does not go into detail. There is no catalogue of household duties and relationships; marriage and sexual morality are not discussed (the seventh commandment is an example at 2.11); the only person to whom the reader is told to be subject is God, in contrast to the detailed codes of subjection in Pauline and Petrine letters. Rather, employers are told to pay wages on the nail (5.4).

He is concerned to avoid sins which divide the community, such as the snobbery which devalues the poor (2.6, 9) or the censoriousness which talks down others in the community (4.11f) and so usurps the role of God's law! Each person is called to be morally responsible, to strengthen his own character (1.4, 5) and look forward to the crown of life, but James has a grasp of how groups and classes of people act wrongly and so threaten their own salvation. The truly religious life is expressed in the way a person treats the destitute (1.27, 2.15f) or manages his business (4.13ff). In the first of these he parallels John's concern that charity matches encouraging words (1 John 3.17f). Another parallel with John is the correction of the erring brother (5.19, *cf* 1 John 5.16, and also *eg* Gal 6.1f). But if James' view is wider than the individual and his household, it does not include the broadest scope which we see in Paul's and Peter's letters, namely the Christian's attitude towards the state, either Jewish or Roman.[26]

James does not denounce Gentile vices, nor recollect the sins from which his readers had been 'saved,' as we find Paul or Peter doing (Rom 1.18–32, 1 Cor 6.9–11, 1 Pet 4.3f). These lists correlate with standard Jewish critiques of Gentile lawlessness, whereas James writes in a Jewish context where 'private' moral values can be taken as read. James' rhetorical stock in trade is more in keeping with Old Testament prophets. Without ignoring vice or jealousy he targets different besetting sins in communities where social injustice needs to be addressed.

So, because of the audience or its early date, James covers only some of the ethical commonplaces of the NT epistles, but does deal in a distinct way with other issues not prominent elsewhere.

---

26 Some scholars link the bias towards the poor in the letter with a supposed reason for James' martyrdom, namely support for poor village priests in Palestine whose revenues were being sequestrated by the rich temple hierarchy (Painter, p 250). But the letter contains no explicit indication of this; its rich are traders or landowners, not temple politicians. But See Davids' suggestion about the *'beth-din'* p 12 above.

James the Catechist?

In his survey of catechetical material (*didache*) in the New Testament letters, E G Selwyn draws James into his view, and finds him using some of the vocabulary common to a series of formulations of instruction for new Christians as the church developed. Common OT texts are used, and common motifs, namely the implications of new birth, renunciation of the evil past, worship, the call to steadfastness and virtues expected of new Christians.[27] At times, however, Selwyn admits that 'James is difficult to bring into the picture here,' (p 407) while some of his connections seem strained (James on worship, for instance (1.27) is decidedly different from any other NT passage. Selwyn, p 403, might better have cited 5.14ff). Selwyn's case for a well thought out body of catechetical teaching early in church history is strong though perhaps over-elaborated. However, it is not so obvious that James was using it, at least in its developed form! Given that Selwyn thought that in any direct relationship between his subject—1 Peter— and James, the latter was derivative (p 463), this is strange. If, however, James is early and such a catechism developed as Selwyn suggests to meet the needs of expanding Gentile missions, we should be less surprised. Indeed, we might ask whether James feeds the catechetical stream very near to source.[28]

---

27 'On the Interrelation of 1 Peter and other NT Epistles'; Essay II appended to his commentary, *The First Epistle of Peter* pp 363–466. He develops earlier work by P Carrington in *The Primitive Christian Catechism*. He sees the apostolic decree of Acts 15 (*c* 49AD) at its first phase with the holiness code of Leviticus central to the model of the church as a new priesthood. Though he recognizes words of Christ within this catechesis, he does not develop the possibility that the form itself dates from before the 40s.

28 Compare Bauckham's correlation of the apostolic decree itself with Leviticus, in *The Book of Acts in its Palestinian Setting*, p 460, citing other authorities.

6
Learning to be Whole

In James we find an expression of how moral character is developed in a community. In a modern writer this would be couched in terms of internalization and reinforcement of behaviour.

After his initial greeting James refers to the trials which his readers face. Challenges to their faith are an everyday fact of life, and they need to learn how to liv—and live joyfully—in such circumstances. This opening gambit is surely significant as the key to the whole letter. Faced with the challenges of life the Christian needs to develop a character which can cope with them, and should aim for a moral and spiritual wholeness (1.4, *teleioi*, perfect, *cf* Mt 5.48, 2 Tim 3.17. Some commentators suggest this implies the perfection of the age to come as a reward, but this overemphasizes the future. It is a quality for now that James commends). Christian character grows under pressure (5.10, 11. *cf* 1 Pet 1.6, 7; 2 Pet 1.5–9; Rom 5.3, 4; *cf* also Jas 1.12 and Mt 5.11, 12), rooted in unwavering faith in God who is reliable.

James is clear that the source of the trials or temptation (*peirasmos* means both) which his readers face is not God himself (1.12ff. Perhaps someone misunderstood the Lord's Prayer. If so, the writer to the Hebrews understands the fatherhood of God in a different light in his theodicy, Heb 12.3–11). Rather human desire (*epithumia*) showing as temptation, grows into sin and so death. The word of God, by contrast, planted in someone's life, is an antidote to human anger and wickedness (1.21). This may be an allusion (perhaps one of the first, for those in the Dead Sea Scrolls are not clear) to the Jewish idea of the *yetser* or inclination; an evil inclination biases the individual towards sin, which he should resist as a moral being, a task in which he is aided by good inclination, variously understood as wisdom, God's spirit, good works, or supremely the *Torah*.[29] However, since Stoic writings use *epithumia* for a force which undermines a man's control of his virtue, Greek ideas possibly supply at least the vocabulary.

He recognizes that to err is human (3.2), but sees this as something inconsistent and unnatural (3.9ff, and see the key word *dipsuchos*—double–minded—in 1.8). His appeal to the way in which the world works is reminiscent of Jesus' appeal to the grapes which do not grow on thorn trees. It is not a formal doctrine of Natural Law, yet is in tune with Jewish appeals to the pattern of creation as a source of moral guidance (*cf* Rom 1.20). This is part of a discussion about the role of speech (3.1–12); he recognizes that what we say becomes what we do, which becomes what we are (3.6). This vicious circle has its origins in hell; it is a false

---

29 See Adamson, pp 65, 70, 79, 354, and Davids, *Commentary*, pp 36f, 83f.

wisdom, which he describes as both belonging to the earth, and demonic (3.15), yet this does not relieve people of moral responsibility. In the next breath he describes jealousy and ambition as the source of evil actions (3.16, *cf* v 14), then lays conflict at the door of 'passions.' These are linked to a friendship with this world, and the devil who is to be resisted. In writing of several sources for wrongdoing James recognizes the interplay in human awareness of what comes from the heart, external influences and spiritual attacks.

Moral Responsibility

Christians have the moral responsibility to resist evil, and so avoid inconsistency in their faith (4.8, *cf* 1.8, 3.11). Moral responsibility is stressed again in James' definition of sin—knowing what to do and not doing it (4.17). This may be a proverb (Origen thought it a 'lost' saying of Jesus) quoted to clinch the argument. If so, it encapsulates James' points from 1.22 onwards, not just 4.13–17 as most commentators think. But is knowledge of what to do derived from gospel law, from what James has just written, or from the exercise of conscience? In the preceding paragraph James expects Christian traders to bring God's providence into their commercial lives as naturally as breathing. The Lord's teaching should be their character and conscience.

This character is internalized by action (1.22ff). The two biggest 'pearls' on James' 'necklace' are the warning against hypocritical partiality in treating rich and poor and the warning against cheap grace, or faith which leads to no tangible action. The public conduct of the church and of individual believers should tally with what they say about love and faith (2.12, 16f).

The direction of our Christian life is set by what we say; the tongue shapes our character, just as a bit directs a horse. Yet, perversely, our speech is often unnatural; we produce good and evil from the same source, in a way that no natural source would do. If unbridled use of the tongue sets off a vicious circle, peaceable wisdom sows the seeds of a virtuous circle in a person's own life, and that of those around him (3.18). In this the virtuous man is not on his own. He can ask God for this wisdom, and is promised that God's grace is there to draw on (4.6–8). He should nevertheless lament and develop a right sense of humility (4.6–12) which shows itself by not setting itself up in judgment over other Christians (see 1 Pet 5.6–9, Rom 14.10–13. Is Paul citing James back at those who think he is their mentor?).

Sticks and Carrots

If this promise of God's grace is not enough, James offers a further incentive to moral conduct—the reality of judgment (4.12) and the coming of the Lord (5.7ff). The tone of these statements is a threat to the unjust, but also an encouragement to the persecuted people of God to remain steadfast.

When James denounces the callous rich (5.1ff), this is not simply radical rhetoric but rational marshalling of evidence, however colourful; the rich will lose what they store because of natural decay, and that decay proves they have more than they need (Schrage, p 293f). They are irrational as well as immoral in retaining what they cannot use. Jesus had taught about storing up treasure (Matt 6.19) but James does not simply pull authority; he combines it with logic and satire and leaves his readers to apply the lesson.[30]

God's support is not mediated unaided. The letter itself is of course an example of the encouragement one Christian gives to others. James envisages teachers (3.1) in the congregations he writes to, and elders and others to whom they can turn for help in a range of circumstances. The final two paragraphs go into fuller detail about this pastoral care of those whose sins and other concerns, need to be dealt with. The moral life is not lived by autonomous individuals, but in a supportive community (which includes the people like us—5.17—from the past who are our exemplars). Mutual confession and prayer are a source of healing, while one Christian may correct another's errors and cover his sins (5.14–16, 19–20). This theme of mutual support and correction, found also in 1 John 5.16, and Gal 6.1ff, evidently formed part of the practice of moral formation of the early church (cf Matt 18.15ff).

In Conclusion

James uses a range of moral discourse. Appeals to authority there are—his own, his Lord's, or the Scriptures' (5.12, 2.8)—but he also invites readers to consider the consequences of behaviour, for their community and in eternity. He wants to see steadfastness in his readers, and warns against double-minded praying or actions by appealing to the consistency seen in creation. He appeals also to the character of God himself (2.5), as well as heroes of faith, to shape his hearers' lifestyle. James knows God's generous grace is a source of the moral energy needed to do right as the church builds towards the moral fulfilment (1.4) which is its goal. Perhaps James does use the 'form' of *paraenesis*. What matters is the content of his letter which uses a range of ethical argument to teach his congregations how to live. He also begins to encourage them to think for themselves (4.15, 'Instead you ought to say…'). James initiates, I suggest, the Christian tradition of writing to build virtuous communities.[31]

---

30 See Adamson, p 264, quoted above, on 'the principle of trajectory.'
31 It is difficult to demonstrate that James (or any other NT writer) is writing for a community without comparing it with the alternatives. Thus for example, though in *Quod omnis probus liber sit* Philo (fl 50CE) describes Essene communities with approval, and extols many of the virtues that James does including the need for action not mere words, its feel is elitist; this is how the noble individual conducts himself.

Appendix 1
James, Paul and Faith versus Works

Luther's description of James as an epistle of straw has cast a shadow over it. His observation needs to be taken in context. Like some modern commentators, he felt that it was thrown together, echoing sayings in Galatians and 1 Peter. He quotes James 2.20 favourably in his *Commentary on Hebrews* (Heb 11.6) where 'dead faith' is criticized. But the greater danger was 'dead works'; he criticizes the Scholastic niceties by which good deeds earn God's approval so that he grants people grace to receive salvation and so do right. He does not suggest that his opponents cited James, but takes James' phrase *sola fide* (2.24) to express his rejection of the Mediaeval Catholic understanding of merit earned by works. That is his usage, not Paul's.[32] In his *Preface to James and Jude* he describes James' ethical purpose and shortcomings: 'He wanted to guard against people who relied on faith without works, but was unequal to the task. He tries to accomplish by harping on the law what the apostles accomplish by stimulating people to love.' James, he adds, cannot be by an apostle; it misinterprets Gen 15.6.

There lies the conundrum. James and Paul use Abraham's faith—or action?—differently, in similar contexts. Is this evidence of a rift or are they independently dealing with different but related issues? The situation between James and Paul was complex. But there is also, I suggest, a 'situation' in recent theology. Hegelian constructs in the 19th Century imagined Jesus' simple thesis overtaken by a Pauline antithesis and synthesized into early catholicism by the likes of Luke. A caricature—but this conflict model still discolours our picture long after Baur's ideas became untenable, so that we read more into genuine differences in the New Testament than was originally there.

But can an ethicist not merely focus on James' moral teaching and ignore this tension within the canon? Not entirely. Ethics is about motives and motivation, as Luther saw, as well as content. If my relationship with God depends on his generosity, received by faith, then I am freed from the fear of not meeting all God's requirements, ritual or moral.[33] But if God's approval depends on ethnicity or on performing certain actions, this causes pride or anxiety about my achievements. At worst other people become means to my ends. Such dangers Paul rejects.

---

32 As Dunn and Suggate point out, he read both Paul and James in the light of his experience of the mediaeval church (*The Justice of God* pp 12ff. For Luther, see *Luther; Early Theological Works* J Atkinson (tr and ed, London: SCM, 1962) pp 209, Hebrews, p 271 (Against the Scholastics) and Heidelberg Theses 3–10; and *Luther's Work* (ed Bachmann, Philadelphia, 1960) vol 54 p 424 (Table Talk) and vol 35, pp 395ff (Preface to James, 1522).

33 Such fear was one feature of Jewish life in James' day. For many Jews obedience to the law was, and is, a joy, but a significant number feared not measuring up. *M Aboth* 2.8–14 lists five pupils of r Johannan b Zakkai, fl 66CE, highlighting their approach to their faith: one betrays this fear. Freed from this, moral behaviour is a question of living out what I have been made, in gratitude and imitation of the Lord (Rom 6.3, 4, 11).

James did not teach that. Ritual observance is dismissed in a couple of scathing verses (1.26f). Knowledge of God's word is his life-giving gift, as is the new birth which results from it. But receiving and believing this word should lead to action, not just study or contemplation. Action shows the belief to be genuine. It is a 'proof of faith' not its alternative. James calls Christians to live by what God has given them and develop a character consistent with that, looking to God's wisdom to enable them. He picks on the defining feature of Jewish belief, the oneness of God revealed in the law, and warns that such credal rectitude, without moral action, is no real faith (2.19, 20). Possessing the gospel-law is nothing if it does not become part of their behaviour (1.24, 25). Grace cannot be cheap.

In one sense it does not matter whether James criticizes a distortion of Pauline teaching (Paul did the same!), or *vice versa*. Both make points relevant to ethical principles and moral action now. These should not be sidelined by a detective story which merely unravels a relationship between two writers. However, as Sanders argued, the time-sequence may influence our application of those points,[34] while the 'faith/works' issue has been central in the interpretation of James and he has been marginalized as a result. It cannot be ignored.

Our primary sources are this letter, Galatians, all of Romans, and perhaps 1 Corinthians. Acts offers a historical framework but is a secondary source. Though it adds significant detail in reporting the 'Council of Jerusalem' and James' role as leader of the Jerusalem church, its chronology is not easy to reconcile with that of Galatians. From Galatians it is clear that debate could be heated, but that Paul went to some lengths to validate his message, and gain James' approval (2.2). Then, as now, people found that difficult to believe, for Paul is clearly not unbiased, but he puts his integrity on the line in stating it (Gal 1.20). They met on two occasions to discuss this. There were those who wanted Paul to include Jewish ritual in his message. On one occasion they came (or claimed to) from James. Paul would not agree. None of this is portrayed as a formal council, and Paul makes no reference to the 'encyclical' of Acts 15.23ff.

There is common ground. Paul was collecting for the poor of Jerusalem as he wrote Romans (15.25ff) and recognized James' concern for the poor (Gal 2.10). The abuses they criticize, however, do not tally. It is kosher food regulations in Corinthians and Romans, or circumcision in Romans and Galatians, which subvert Paul's gospel to the nations, whereas the works which James advocates are (in modern terms) moral, not ceremonial. The empty faith which he criticizes may be an 'only-believeism' which claimed Paul as its mentor, but it does not correspond to the antinomian errors which Paul denounced (Rom 6.1). Neither directly criticizes the other's teaching (or both missed the point totally! This is hard to believe given that they met to understand each other). Romans, however, reads to me as a 'position statement' written with a knowledge of James. That view is not

---

34 See above, p 6.

general; more scholars see James as a riposte to a Pauline outlook.[35]

One explanation claims that 'James' was written in the sub-apostolic era, to recall the church from a degenerate, morally lazy Paulinism. But its use of Gospel material appears to be from an early stage of transmission. Therefore it is proposed that the letter was ghost-written posthumously in good Greek, using genuine Jacobean material, to apply his teaching to a changed world.[36] A key argument is that James' use of 'faith' must depend on Paul's earlier usage.

But must we postulate Paul, even misunderstood, to understand James? 'Faith' was not invented by Paul, nor was he the first to look back on Abraham as an exemplar! We find faith discussed in relation to works in Wisdom 3.9, 14, in a way which tallies well with James' points. Philo (*de Abrahamo* 270–274) discusses how Abraham's faith was shown and pleased God, while he quotes Gen 15.6 as proof that trust in God, rather than reason or conjecture, is the best grounding for life (*Legum Allegoriae* III 228). In 1 Maccabees (2.52, 61) the importance of faith in God is stressed, and Abraham's faithfulness when tested receives prominent treatment. m Aboth 5.3 highlights the ten trials of Abraham. None of these examples reveals the aberration which James criticizes, but the significance of faith was part of James' ambience. For the distortions he criticizes we might compare John the Baptist's denunciations of those who said 'We have Abraham for our father,' or the conversation of John 8.39ff. The Rabbis pick up the significance of Abraham's testing and sacrifice on Mt Moriah, though their developed use of his merit in the story may be a response to Christian claims.[37] Furthermore, early Judaism discussed how law and kindness, study and action interrelated (m Aboth 1.2, 17; 2.1; 3.16).

In brief, there is more behind Paul's or James' discussion of faith, works and Abraham than is found merely in either of them. James makes sense without Paul, though Paul is aware of James' views, hijacked by others (Rom 4.1. Paul appears to be picking up *someone else's* point as at 6.1).

A Tentative Scenario

Preaching in Cilicia in the 40s Paul is aware of misunderstanding of his interpretation of the gospel bypassing Jewish regulations. As the 'junior partner' in the enterprise—which we forget with our hindsight—he attempts to get an *imprimatur* from James and Peter, and after some opposition receives a *nihil obstat* (Gal 2.1–10). James meanwhile is concerned for scattered Jewish Christians, and their tendency to rest on their laurels (whether 'faith' or Jewishness). He may be aware of Paul's angle before their meeting, but if James is written about this time it is not

---

35 Summaries in Painter, p 238ff, or Chester p 49ff. I find my conclusions supported by Robinson, *Redating* p 127f. There appears a curious blindness to this work of Robinson on the part of subsequent scholars. It is not so much refuted as ignored.

36 R P Martin, quoted by Painter p 242, and Painter himself p 245ff, proposing Luke as the ghost-writer, inverting the argument based on similarities between Acts 15 and James. On 'Q' see P J Hartin, cited above.

37 S W Baron, *A Social and Religious History of the Jews*, vol II p 138. Compare William Barclay, *The Gospel of Matthew* vol I, p 39. Most Rabbis cited are 2nd or 3rd century CE, and Baron points out that they may be using the sacrifice of Isaac to counter Christian teaching. See *eg* m Aboth 5.2, 3.

written against Paul, for its concerns are morals not ceremonies.

After Paul and James have reached their understanding people who apply James' line to ceremonial bring out problems at Antioch (Gal 2.11ff, *cf* Acts 15.1ff). Shortly afterwards they or people like them surface in Galatia, and (before the meeting in Jerusalem; Acts 15.6ff) Paul dashes off Galatians in exasperation, emphasizing James' *nihil obstat*, and turning some of his catch phrases against his supposed partisans ('God shows no partiality' Gal 2.6, compare Jas 2.1, 9; Acts 10.34, and perhaps 'fruit,' Gal 5.22, compare Jas 3.18). So far he has not seen James' letter, perhaps because it was not written until now (but not later or it would deal with points raised at the Jerusalem council). It is a 'position statement' and responds to other people not met elsewhere in our surviving literature.

Following the Jerusalem Council Paul continues his missionary work, incorporating a collection for the poor (Acts 11.27ff, Gal 2.10, 1 Cor 16.1). In the course of this he writes his own position paper to the Roman Church. He has seen or heard James by this time and uses it approvingly while subtly correcting it, intending not to undermine James himself but those who misapply his arguments to urge Jewish ceremonial law on the Gentile church. This makes most sense of the way one letter echoes the other.[38]

Referring to Abraham he gently corrects the understanding of faith found in James and most Jewish sources. In James the time sequence between Abraham's 'work' of offering his son (Jas 2.21, *cf* Gen 22.9 and m Aboth V 2, 3) and God's assessment of him as righteous (Jas 2.23, *cf* Gen 15.6) is ignored. Paul uses the events in their recorded sequence (Rom 4.3, 4.10) but, since he is not disagreeing with James' views on faithful obedience, but with people who champion ritual observance, he highlights Abraham's circumcision as coming after commendation for his faith. Elsewhere in the letter he explains that he has not reneged on his Jewishness (*cf* Acts 21.17–26).[39]

This reconstruction implies that James is not a pale sub-apostolic echo of ideas found in earlier letters but is itself the work of a pioneer. He translated his Lord's teaching and Jewish virtues of steadfastness and faith in the face of trials into the beginnings of a Christian ethic of virtue and delight in the royal Law of the gospel. If it seems tame by comparison with some of Paul's ethics, or Peter's, it is not because it is an inferior copy but because it is the first attempt, which others built on.

---

38 I have already noted Rom 4.1 and 14.10, 13; in Rom 2.13 Paul, approvingly, uses the words *poietes* and *akroates* ('doer' and 'hearer') in tandem. They appear in Jas 1.22, 25, but in this sense nowhere else in surviving Greek literature. In Rom 2.11 Paul uses the word *prosopolempsia*—partiality, another near-solecism. His use is different from Jas 2.1ff, but makes sense as an allusion to James' point, reapplied to God's acceptance of Gentiles as well as the poor. In Rom 5.3ff. Paul uses an escalade of virtues focused on *hypomone*—stickability—and *dokime*—proven character—echoing Jas 1.12. Of the two, *James* is the less developed. Paul pays tribute to James' seminal work in developing a Christian response to hardship by alluding to him. Abraham, he drops in, did not *waver* in his faith (Rom 4.20)—he was an example of the unwavering faith which James commends (Jas 1.6 *cf* 3.17). Again he uses James with approval.

39 See discussion in Bauckham, 'James and the Jerusalem Church' p 475ff.

Appendix 2
Bibliography

Adamson, J B, *James, the Man and his Message* (Grand Rapids: Eerdmans, 1982)

Adamson, J B, *The Epistle of James* (NICNT, Grand Rapids: Eerdmans, 1976)

Baron, S W, *A Social and Religious History of the Jews* (New York: Columbia UP, 1952)

Bauckham, R, 'James and the Jerusalem Church' in *The Book of Acts in its First Century Setting, vol 4* Bauckham, R (ed), (Carlisle: Paternoster, 1995)

Bauckham, R, *James: Wisdom of James, disciple of Jesus the Sage*, (NT Readings, London: Routledge, 1999).

Bauckham, R, *Jude and the Relatives of Jesus in the Early Church* (Edin: T & T Clark, 1990).

Bauer, Arndt and Gindrich, *A Greek-English Lexicon of the New Testament* (Cambridge, 1952).

Carrington, P, *The Primitive Christian Catechism* (Cambridge: CUP, 1940)

Chester, A, and Martin, R P, *The Theologies of the Letters of James, Peter and Jude* (Cambridge: CUP, 1994).

Danby, H, (trans), *The Mishnah* (Cambridge: CUP, 1933).

Davids, P H, *The Epistle of James* (NIGTC, Carlisle: Paternoster, 1982).

Dibelius, M, *Der Brief des Jacobus* (Gottingen, 11th edition, 1964).

Dunn, J D G, and Suggate, A M, *The Justice of God* (Carlisle: Paternoster, 1993).

Edgar, D H, *Has God not Chosen the Poor?* (Sheffield: SAP, 2001).

Guthrie, D, *New Testament Introduction: Hebrews to Revelation* (London: Tyndale, 1964).

Hartin, P J, *James and the Q-Sayings of Jesus* (Sheffield: SAP, 1991).

Hays, R B, *The Moral Vision of the New Testament* (Edinburgh: T & T Clark, 1996).

Houlden, J L, *Ethics in the New Testament* (Edinburgh: T & T Clark, 1992, 1975).

Laws, S, (née Marshall) *Commentary on the Epistle of James* (London: A & C Black, 1980).

Luther, M, *Luther's Work*, Bachmann et al (eds) (Philadelphia, 1960) vols 35, 54.

Luther, M, *Luther, Early Theological Works*, Atkinson, J (ed) (London: SCM Press, 1962).

MacIntyre, A, *A Short History of Ethics* (London: RKP, 1967).

Martin, R P, *James* (Word Biblical Commentary, Waco, 1988).

Mayor, J B, *The Epistle of St James* (London, 1913).

Mitton, C L, *The Epistle of James* (London: Marshall, Morgan & Scott, 1966).

Moo, D J, *The Letter of James* (TNTC, Leicester: IVP, 1985).

Moo, D J, *The Letter of James* (Pillar, Leicester: Apollos, 2000).

Painter, J, *Just James, the Brother of Jesus in History and Tradition* (Edinburgh: T & T Clark, 1999).

Philo, The works of, Tr C D Yonge (1854), D M Scholer (ed), (Hendrickson, 1993).

Robinson, J A T, *Redating the New Testament* (London: SCM Press, 1976).

Sanders, J T, *Ethics in the New Testament* (London: SCM Press, 1975).

Schrage, W, *The Ethics of the New Testament* (Tr D E Green, Edinburgh: T & T Clark, 1988).

Selwyn, E G, *The First Epistle of Peter* (London: MacMillan, 1947).

Tasker, R V G, *The General Epistle of James* (London: Tyndale, 1957).

Wachob, W H, *The Voice of Jesus in the Social Rhetoric of James* (Cambridge: CUP, 2001).

Witherington, Ben III, *The Jesus Quest* (Carlisle: Paternoster, 1995).